EXPLORING WORLD CULTURES

# Australia

Alicia Z. Klepeis

Cavendish
Square

New York

Published in 2018 by Cavendish Square Publishing, LLC
243 5th Avenue, Suite 136, New York, NY 10016

Copyright © 2018 by Cavendish Square Publishing, LLC

First Edition

Library of Congress Cataloging-in-Publication Data

Names: Klepeis, Alicia, 1971- author.
Title: Australia / Alicia Z. Klepeis.
Description: New York : Cavendish Square Publishing, [2018] |
Series: Exploring world cultures | Includes index.
Identifiers: LCCN 2017013865 (print) | LCCN 2017013950 (ebook) |
ISBN 9781502630148 (E-book) | ISBN 9781502630131 (library bound) |
ISBN 9781502630117 (pbk.) | ISBN 9781502630124 (6 pack)
Subjects: LCSH: Australia--Juvenile literature.
Classification: LCC DU96 (ebook) | LCC DU96 .K54 2018 (print) | DDC 994--dc23
LC record available at https://lccn.loc.gov/2017013865

Editorial Director: David McNamara
Editor: Kristen Susienka
Copy Editor: Alex Tessman
Associate Art Director: Amy Greenan
Designer: Graham Abbott
Production Coordinator: Karol Szymczuk
Photo Research: J8 Media

Printed in the United States of America

# Contents

# Introduction

Australia is an island. It is also a country. Australia is located in **Oceania**. It has lots of special traditions and celebrations.

Two Aboriginal children have fun.

Australia has a long and rich history. Its people come from all over the world. The country's government is a **democracy**.

People in Australia work many kinds of jobs. Some are farmers or national park rangers. Others are bankers, hotel managers, or teachers. Miners gather minerals from under the ground. Some people make chemicals and machines.

Australia has some incredible places to visit, like deserts, beaches, mountains, and rain forests. It is also known for its unusual animals and plants. Australian families often enjoy camping and spending time in nature.

Australians like to play sports. They also value music, literature, and other types of art. Australia is a fascinating country to explore.

Visitors enjoy a campfire in Yanga National Park.

# Geography

Australia is a little smaller than the continental United States. It covers 2,969,975 square miles (7,692,202 square kilometers).

A map of Australia

Australia is the only country in the world that is also a continent. It is the largest island in the world. This huge island lies between the Indian Ocean and the Pacific Ocean.

Most of Australia is flat, but the country does have some mountains. The Blue and Snowy Mountains are two examples. The Great Dividing Range stretches for 2,300 miles (3,700 kilometers) through eastern and southeastern Australia.

## Plants and Animals

Many plants and animals in Australia are only found here. Unique species include the echidna, platypus, and the rainbow lorikeet. Eucalyptus and banksia trees grow here.

Here stand two adult kangaroos and a baby.

More than one-third of Australia is desert. In many parts of the country, water is scarce. The climate is more comfortable in southeastern and southwestern Australia. Most people live in these areas. Much of northern Australia has a tropical climate.

FACT!

Australia does not share any land borders with other countries.

7

# History

The first people arrived in Australia about fifty thousand years ago. These early people lived off the land. They learned to survive in

This sketch shows how Sydney Cove looked in 1788.

the harsh Australian outback, or dry desert lands.

In the early 1600s, European explorers arrived. In 1770, Captain James Cook made maps of the east coast of Australia. He claimed this territory for England.

Beginning in 1788, Britain started six colonies in Australia. Many of the early settlers were criminals or prisoners from British jails. At first, relations between the Europeans and

After gold was discovered in Victoria, Australia, in 1851, people rushed there hoping to find a fortune.

the **Aboriginal** people were peaceful. But these groups had conflict over who owned the land.

In 1901, the six colonies in Australia joined together. They formed the **Commonwealth** of Australia. The six colonies became states. During the twentieth century, people moved to Australia from all over the world.

## Neville Bonner

In 1971, Neville Bonner became the first Aboriginal person to serve in Australia's parliament. He fought for the rights of native peoples.

Senator Neville Bonner in 1979

Australia is a democracy, but the country is also part of the British Commonwealth. That means the head of state is actually the king or queen of England. The prime minister is in charge of running Australia's government.

Australia's Parliament House

Australia is divided into six states and two territories. The country's capital is Canberra.

Australia's government has three parts:

• legislative: This part of the government is called Parliament. People in Parliament write new

**FACT!**

All Australian citizens over the age of eighteen must vote in elections.

laws, give money to the government, and make sure laws are followed.

• judicial: The courts make up this part of the government. They follow the country's constitution.

• executive: The prime minister, deputy prime minister, **governor-general**, and **cabinet** make up this part of the government.

Australia's parliament has two parts: the Senate and the House of Representatives. The Senate has 76 members. The House of Representatives has 150 members. Both houses meet in Parliament House in the city of Canberra to pass laws.

## A Female Leader

Julia Gillard was the first female prime minister of Australia. She was in office from 2010 to 2013.

Australia has one of the biggest economies in the world. Its most important trading partners include China, Japan, the United States, and South Korea. Its currency is called the Australian dollar.

A close-up of Australian dollar coins and notes (bills)

Australian factories make many different products, like wool, aluminum, and machines. The country is also rich in natural resources. Miners dig minerals like gold, copper, and coal from under the earth's surface.

About three out of four Australian workers have service jobs. Some people work in schools,

In 2016, over eight million tourists visited Australia from other countries.

stores, or parks. Others have jobs in hotels, hospitals, and other businesses.

In the countryside, farmers grow many crops. Wheat, barley, and sugarcane are a few examples. They also grow many kinds of fruits, like bananas, mangoes, and pineapples. Australia is an important producer of meat and wine.

## Cattle Station

Australia is home to the world's largest cattle station, Anna Creek Station. It gives many people jobs. It is in South Australia.

# The Environment

The animals, plants, and people of Australia need clean water and air to live. Some places in the country don't have these things. Compared to many other countries,

Bush fires rage through the Australian outback.

Australia has clean air. But that doesn't mean there is no air pollution here. Some of the pollution comes from cars, trucks, or coal.

One of the biggest challenges for Australia concerns water. Why? The country often suffers from droughts. This also can cause huge wildfires that destroy people's homes and animals' habitats.

Australia is home to many endangered animals, including the mountain pygmy possum and the orange-bellied parrot.

Some parts of Australia have had trouble with soil **erosion**. Cattle chew up the plants. This can cause the soil to blow away. Without enough soil, the land is not good for growing crops.

## Energy Sources

Solar panels in northern Australia

Australia gets more than three-quarters of its energy from fossil fuels, like coal or oil. The country wants to increase its production of clean energy sources. It is starting to use waterpower and solar energy more.

Today, over twenty-two million people live in Australia. The country's population is one of the most diverse in the world.

Over 25 percent of the people living in Australia were born

This 1913 photo shows a ship bringing people from England to Australia.

in other nations. Many came from the United Kingdom and other European countries. This was especially true when Australia was in its early days and needed people to settle and work the land.

People have also come to Australia from New Zealand, Asia, North Africa, and the Middle East.

16

Many immigrants arrived after World War II. In the 1970s, lots of refugees from southeast Asia traveled to Australia. They left war-torn areas in search of a better life. All of these newcomers brought their own foods, languages, and traditions to Australia.

## Australia's First Peoples

About 3 percent of Australia's population is made up of native peoples: the Aborigines and the Torres Strait Islanders.

Over 89 percent of Australia's people live in cities and towns. These cities tend to be along the coast. Some city people live in apartments. Others live in houses. Australians in the city might drive to work or they might ride the bus or

Commuters board a bus in Kellyville, a suburb of Sydney.

take the train to their jobs. It's common for families in cities to have cell phones and computers.

Life in Australia's countryside often has a slower pace than in the cities. Farmers grow all

The outback town of Coober Pedy has homes, hotels, and restaurants underground. This helps people beat the extreme heat there!

This is the kitchen area of an underground home in Coober Pedy.

kinds of crops. Ranchers raise cattle and sheep. Some Australians work as miners. Others have jobs at wildlife parks or other tourist attractions.

## Women in Australia

Just like in the United States, many women in Australia work outside of the home. They are lawyers, doctors, businesswomen, teachers, and more.

# Religion

Australia has no official religion. All people are free to believe in what they want. However, religion is important to many Australians.

St. Patrick's Cathedral in Melbourne

Nearly 60 percent are Christian. Slightly more than half of these Christians are Protestant. Most of the rest are Roman Catholic. Christian church services are typically held every Sunday. Some people attend every week, but most do not. Australian Christians, like others around the globe, celebrate certain holidays like Christmas and Easter.

Many religions besides Christianity are practiced in Australia. Nearly 3 percent of

More than 22 percent of Australians don't follow any religion.

Australians are members of the Orthodox Church. More than 2 percent follow Islam and Buddhism. The fastest-growing religion in Australia in recent decades is Hinduism. This religion has its roots in South Asia and is popular in India.

Dreamtime is the subject of this Aboriginal dot painting.

## Aboriginal Beliefs

Australia's Aboriginal people have their own religious beliefs. Each tribe has its own beliefs and legends about Dreamtime, or the Creation Period.

# Language

Australia does not have an official language. However, English is the most commonly spoken language in Australia. It is the language most used by the country's government, schools, and businesses.

A young woman in Sydney's Chinatown

Some Australians speak languages other than English. Immigrants who have come to Australia from around the

FACT!

Some Aboriginal words that became part of the English vocabulary include boomerang, kangaroo, and koala.

Want to talk like an Australian? "Lollies" are candy or sweets, "barbie" is a barbeque, and "G'day" means hello.

world often speak different languages. More than 1 percent of the country's population speaks each of the following languages: Mandarin, Italian, Arabic, Greek, Cantonese, and Vietnamese.

Kids in Australia often learn foreign languages at school. Schools here offer a variety of languages, including Japanese, French, and various Aboriginal languages. In some parts of Australia, classes are taught in Aboriginal languages and the students learn English as their second language.

# Arts and Festivals

People in Australia enjoy arts of all kinds. Aboriginal artists are known for their own style of painting, often called dot art. Some paintings show Dreamtime stories from different Aboriginal groups. Clifford Possum Tjapaltjarri is a famous Aboriginal artist.

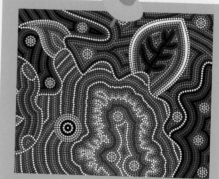

This illustration shows bush fires. It is based on an Aboriginal-style dot painting.

## Australia Day

January 26 is Australia Day. This holiday marks the beginning of British occupation in Australia. Today people celebrate their nation with fireworks, concerts, and barbeques.

**FACT!**

Many famous actors come from Australia. They include Cate Blanchett, Nicole Kidman, Hugh Jackman, and Geoffrey Rush.

Ken Done is another Australian painter. His artwork uses bright colors. It often shows Australian landmarks and animals.

Music is also an important part of Australian culture. Popular bands from Australia are Men at Work, AC/DC, Midnight Oil, and Silverchair. The didgeridoo is a traditional Aboriginal instrument. It's a long wind instrument made of wood.

There are holidays and festivals in Australia throughout the year. Anzac Day is April 25. On this day, Australians celebrate a historical military achievement in 1915.

Many Australian people enjoy sports. One of the most popular sports is Australian Rules Football, or "footy." This sport is played by two teams of eighteen players each on an oval-shaped field. Players aim to get the ball through posts at the ends of the field.

James Kelly (*left*) escapes being tackled during a 2011 Australian Football League match.

Snorkeling and scuba diving on the Great Barrier Reef attract people from around the globe.

## Basketball Players

Several popular basketball players come from Australia. They include Kyrie Irving, Andrew Bogut, Ben Simmons, and Patty Mills.

Soccer and cricket are also well liked in Australia. People use a bat and ball to play cricket. This game came to Australia with the British settlers.

Australians love to spend time near the water. Swimming and surfing are popular with families and athletes.

Many Australian people like to play games. Outdoor games include lawn bowling, jumping rope, and handball. Card games and board games are also popular with kids of all ages.

# Food

Australians eat many different kinds of food. Shrimp, salmon, shark, and oysters are popular choices.

In addition to fish dishes, people in Australia like meat, including beef and lamb. Roast lamb is the national dish. Meat pie is also a favorite. Many Australians cook meals that include chicken.

People in Australia enjoy eating many different fruits. Passion fruit and papayas are popular here. Adults often drink tea, coffee, and wine. Many kids

## FACT!

Vegemite is one of Australia's most famous foods. It's a salty, dark brown paste usually eaten on bread.

Foods found in the outback are called bush tucker. Sweet honey ants and wichetty grubs are just two examples.

enjoy sweet drinks like fruit squash or cordial.

What do Australians like for dessert? Lamingtons are cakes covered in chocolate and coconut and pavlova is a meringue-like treat often served with fruit.

A raspberry, banana, and passion fruit pavlova is decorated to celebrate Australia Day.

# Glossary

**Aboriginals**   The native peoples of Australia.

**cabinet**   People who help the leader of a government.

**Commonwealth**   Independent countries once part of the British Empire.

**democracy**   A system of government where citizens choose their leaders.

**erosion**   Wearing down objects by wind or water brushing against them for a long time.

**governor-general**   A person who takes the place of the English king or queen in important meetings in Australia.

**Oceania**   An area that includes the islands of the Pacific Ocean and adjacent seas.

# Find Out More

## Books

Hirsch, Rebecca E. *Australia*. Rookie Read-About
Geography. New York: Scholastic, 2012.

Sexton, Colleen. *Australia*. Exploring Countries.
Minneapolis, MN: Bellwether Media, 2016.

## Website

**National Geographic Kids: Australia**

http://kids.nationalgeographic.com/explore/
countries/australia

## Video

**What Is in Australia?**

https://www.youtube.com/watch?v=nSsvQp-70p4

This video talks about a number of Australian
animals, including dingos, platypuses, and koalas.

# Index

# About the Author

**Alicia Z. Klepeis** began her career at the National Geographic Society. She is the author of many kids' books, including *Haunted Cemeteries Around the World*, *Bizarre Things We've Called Medicine*, and *A Time for Change*. She lived for two years in Wollongong, Australia.